Budgies
...getting started

EVELYN MILLER

CONTENTS

© T.F.H. Publications, Inc.

Distributed in the UNITED STATES to the Pet Trade by T.F.H. Publications, Inc., 1 TFH Plaza, Neptune City, NJ 07753; on the Internet at www.tfh.com; in CANADA by Rolf C. Hagen Inc., 3225 Sartelon St., Montreal, Quebec H4R 1E8; Pet Trade by H & L Pet Supplies Inc., 27 Kingston Crescent, Kitchener, Ontario N2B 2T6; in ENGLAND by T.F.H. Publications, PO Box 74, Havant PO9 5TT; in AUSTRALIA AND THE SOUTH PACIFIC by T.F.H. (Australia), Pty. Ltd., Box 149, Brookvale 2100 N.S.W., Australia; in NEW ZEALAND by Brooklands Aquarium Ltd., 5 McGiven Drive, New Plymouth, RD1 New Zealand; in SOUTH AFRICA by Rolf C. Hagen S.A. (PTY.) LTD., P.O. Box 201199, Durban North 4016, South Africa; in JAPAN by T.F.H. Publications, Japan—Jiro Tsuda, 10-12-3 Ohjidai, Sakura, Chiba 285, Japan. Published by T.F.H. Publications, Inc.
    MANUFACTURED IN THE UNITED STATES OF AMERICA BY T.F.H. PUBLICATIONS, INC.

Budgies are the world's most popular pet bird.

What other little bird is such a dynamic economic force? Perhaps as many as a million budgerigars are bred and sold every year.

Seed is carefully prepared, not only for his nutrition but for his epicurean palate. Furniture and toys are made just for him. Architects design his cages. Doctors prepare his remedies. Language records are pressed. Associations are formed. And books, like this, are written. All because America has fallen in love with this charming little bird.

And why not? There is no pet easier to care for and take to your heart. He's as beautiful as a rainbow! Spirited and playful! Entertaining! And most wonderful of all, he can be taught to talk!

As with any pet, your parakeet reflects his surroundings. Make life happy and healthy for him, and he'll reward you with thousands

of hours of fun and pleasure.

Can you imagine a tiny little bird becoming a member of the family? You'll see! He'll join you at coffee. He'll break in on your telephone conversations. He'll sit on your shoulder and watch TV. He'll ride on your dog's head. He'll ride on *your* head. He'll admire himself in a mirror for hours. He loves company and company will love him!

Many people buy their parakeet a companion. "He needs a friend," they say. Really, I believe that what these people honestly want is just another parakeet. Can you blame them?

For such a little bird, hardly bigger than a finch, this graceful, beautifully colored member of the parrot family has been burdened with a lot of names. Scientists call him *Melopsittacus undulatus.* But the great variety of popular names bestowed on him over the years has led to endless confusion. To list only a few, he is known as the shell, zebra, undulated or warbling grass parakeet, or the canary parrot. In Great Britain and by many American hobbyists he is commonly called a budgerigar, or budgie. There is only one name he is not: a lovebird, although for many years he was mistakenly called that. Today the name "lovebird" is reserved for a stocky African bird, heavier than the parakeet, with a short stubby tail.

The term "parakeet" is an anglicizing of the French name for the bird: *paroquette* meaning "little parrot." The descriptive names "zebra," "undulated" and "shell" refer to the

Mirrors fascinate budgies.

Budgies and other pets can be trained to get along well together...but the relationship can never be 100% reliable.

5

Budgies originally came from Australia, but they never came in this color. Budgies have been bred in dozens of colors and color patterns.

bird's distinctive markings: a striped or sea-shell pattern of black across its head, neck and wings. "Budgerigar" is an anglicizing of the Australian bushmen's name for the bird, "betcherrygar," which can be roughly translated as "pretty good eating." Roughly translated, indeed--others give the aborigines more credit for an appreciation of beauty and translate the term as "pretty bird."

The parakeet's native home is Australia. There he gathers with thousands of his own kind into large migratory flocks and nests twice a year, in the spring and the autumn. He lives off the wild grasses, their seeds, and the scrub vegetation of the dry grasslands. He was living there by the millions when first seen and described by two exploring English naturalists, Shaw and Gould.

This was early in the nineteenth century when "as many as fifty thousand birds rose in green-and-yellow clouds."

It was not until 1840 that Englishmen were to see their first live budgerigar; before then the birds had been exhibited only in museums as rare specimens, "stuffed." In 1837 Gould wrote in a book all that he then knew about *Melopsittacus undulatus* (he was the one who gave the bird its Latin name), and

ended by saying, "Of its nest, eggs, etc., nothing is known." How ironic it is to realize that within only a few generations even young children would have firsthand knowledge of parakeets and their breeding habits.

Gould's brother-in-law, Charles Coxen, hand-reared these first birds, and before long they were being bred successfully in captivity. It was then believed that they had to be kept in pairs, that one alone would pine away and die. It was for this reason they became known as lovebirds and their amazing ability to mimic and talk took a long time to

Young birds have striped foreheads. As they mature, they lose these stripes.

Budgies are easily tamed and trained so they won't bite your finger.

become known.

But even though parakeets could be bred in captivity, it was cheaper and easier to trap wild ones and ship them from Australia. So rapidly were the flocks being depleted that Australia finally had to pass a law forbidding their export. But this created no great problem. Parakeets bred under domesticated conditions are far superior in size and color and are healthier than their wild

cousins. Aviaries soon began to appear all over Europe.

It wasn't long before an occasional mutation began to turn up. These were birds of different coloring. Soon breeders began to discover that they could produce many various-hued birds by selective mating. A light yellow appeared in 1875. Skyblue ones appeared about ten years later.

France created olive-green birds during the First World War. And the beautiful cobalt blues were first bred in 1920 by crossing skyblues with olive greens.

The cobalts created a great fuss in Japan. In 1925, a Japanese prince was intrigued by a pair of them he saw in England. He took them back to Japan as a gift to his sweetheart. This started a hysterical craze. Every Japanese had to give a pair of the beautiful blue birds to his beloved. English breeders were not able to keep up with the demand; in 1927 one pair sold for $1,000. The craze continued until Japanese breeders got into the act and bred cobalts by the thousands. Soon with the help of a law forbidding any further imports, the

Budgies kept in a group are very difficult to tame. It is also very difficult to control the quality and quantity of their breeding. You never know which pair produced which young.

A pair of budgies can be very loving... perhaps that's why they are often mistakenly referred to as *lovebirds*.

prices dropped to somewhere within reason. In addition, a disastrous earthquake in 1927 caused a shortage of "wild" money, even among the aristocracy and the rich. Parakeets returned to the cages of the original fancier, the common man, at prices he could afford.

By the late 1920's the parakeet had found its way into America's heart, and profes-sional breeding began. Another boom in popularity occurred in the 1950's. Estimates were that the number of parakeets in the country went from a few million to over ten million in just a decade. Almost all parakeets in the United States are "home-bred," which provides enough of every kind of parakeet for every fancier.

Look closely! This is a young bird because the stripes are still visible on the forehead. The cere (nostrils) are blue. Usually this indicates a male....but look closely. Did you ever think a bird could have eyelashes?

Color Varieties

Budgerigars are extremely colorful. Everyone of their feathers is colored. Yet, when inbred mutants are propagated, the results produced more than 70 distinct color varieties. A color variety is recognized when the strain is fixed and breeders are able to replicate it.

The color of the wild budgerigar as it exists in Australia is light green with a yellow head—"a saucy yellow face," said one writer—and black and yellowish seashell-like markings on the wings. In captivity, parakeets have been bred in green, yellow, blue, white, gray, violet, and in every hue and combination of these colors. At this writing there are more than 70 *recognized* color varieties; there are many others which have not been recognized because they do not "breed true"—that is, their offspring do not appear to follow the accepted Mendelian laws. All these colors have sprung from the original green bird. The unexpected color variations were noted by breeders and

Right: This green budgie is starting to molt. It loses its feathers slowly, replacing them with new feathers.

Facing page: This magnificent bird is a show quality budgie. This male is quite mature and should not be selected either as a pet or for breeding purposes because of its age. But it is such a quality bird that you MIGHT want to take a chance in using it for breeding purposes.

then established by selective breeding according to the laws of heredity.

All of the colors that have so far appeared are combinations of yellow and black pigments and a blue color effect, which is not a true pigment. That is why we have yet to see our first red or pink parakeet. It is not impossible, however, that someday a red mu-tant will turn up. After many years it was discovered that the canary could be successfully crossed with a red South American siskin. So far no closely related bird with red plumage that is small enough to mate with a parakeet has

been discovered.

Some of the newer colors are the graywings, cinnamons, lutinos, albinos, opalines, buttercups, yellow-faced blues, fallows, violets and mauves. The colors come in these principal patterns: normal, opaline, rainbow and pied (This list is by no means complete).

Apparently, however, the so-called "average" parakeet buyer prefers the more common colors. The pet department of a large department store discovered that their customers' first choice was blue, with green second, and yellow third; all of the other colors were much poorer sellers.

This is a show quality lutino.

Choosing your Parakeet

Don't dash to your pet shop and buy the first cute bird you see. Choosing a parakeet is not difficult, but there are a few factors which should be taken into consideration--sex, color, age, and health, for instance--and I suggest that before starting out to purchase your new pet you either commit the more important of these "do's and don'ts" to memory or jot them down on a slip of paper to take along.

HOW MANY?

First of all, make up your mind if you want just one bird, a pair (male and female), two birds of the same sex, or enough to set you up in business as a breeder.

If you've never owned a parakeet before, let me suggest that you start out with one young bird less than three months old. He will be easier to tame and train because if he has no bird for company he will devote all of his attention and affection to you. As for teaching a parakeet to talk, it is difficult to do if he has a bird companion.

If you are considering two birds because you have the mistaken idea that parakeets are "love birds" and will pine away in loneliness if not kept in pairs, forget it. You are going to provide all the companionship your bird needs.

If you are considering a *pair* with the thought in the back of your mind that eventually they will mate and bless your home with a lot of little keets, forget that too. A single pair of keets

Selecting your budgie requires you to make up your mind about how many budgies you want, whether or not you want to breed them, whether you want to train and tame them, and how much you want to spend. The rarity of the bird's color and its pedigree have almost no direct correlation to the bird's pet quality.

Choosing your Parakeet

Budgies can live to 15 years of age if properly cared for; therefore it is worthwhile to tame and train them as soon as possible.

kept as pets in a cage rarely breed. If you're lucky (or unlucky, depending upon your point of view) it may happen, but the odds are against it. Parakeets that have been tamed and trained do not make good breeders. They seem to lose all of their parental instincts and even when eggs are laid do not know how to incubate them or care for their young.

The average parakeet's life span is from twelve to fifteen years. Parakeet breeding has developed in the United States to the point where there are many large-scale breeders producing good-quality birds at reasonable prices. Our breeders have learned by now to choose their breeding stock carefully so that the birds you purchase are of excellent quality.

There are, however, a couple of ways to save money. Males are sometimes priced higher than females. This is because some people think, mistakenly, that males make the better talkers. They are wrong. A female makes an equally good pet, just as tameable, just as talkative. Also, finger-tamed pets usually cost more because someone has taken the time to start their training. However, since any parakeet less than three months old can be quickly and easily tamed, buying a "hand-raised" pet is a needless luxury. Even adult birds—and they are the least expensive of all unless trained—can with patience eventually be tamed.

WHICH SEX?

Sex should not be a consideration unless you are planning to mate your pet. With some varieties the male's hue is darker than the female's, but the feathers of both are equally brilliant. Both can be trained to become expert talkers and do tricks; both will be equally loved. Young females are inclined to be more aggressive than males and more inquisitive, and they take longer to become accustomed to you and are noisier. So it's about six of one and half a dozen of the other.

Some say the aggressiveness of the baby female is useful when it comes to distinguishing the sexes. The female when first handled is likely to bite harder than the young male. Also baby females have a tendency to "cluck" softly when bothered.

Over the upper part of the beak is a wax-like band of flesh, the "cere." It surrounds the nostrils, and from its color you can determine the sex of the mature bird. The cere of the male is deep blue; the female's is a whitish tan,

These two birds are young enough to be tamed and trained easily. The blue bird is older than the green one as evidenced by the disappearing stripes on the forehead.

This beautiful normal violet budgie is of show quality.

pink, light blue or brown. Distinguishing the sex of young birds is just about impossible because the cere's color is similar in both males and females until they're eight to ten weeks old, although the young male's cere is apt to be slightly plumper and more pronounced. At about twelve weeks the cere of the male begins to turn blue, eventually becoming bright blue. The cere of the female gradually turns whitish and then becomes tan when she's about a year old. When she's ready to breed it turns a dark brown.

HOW OLD?

Choose a bird between six weeks and three months old, the younger the better if you want a bird that can most easily be tamed, trained, and taught to talk (But never less than six weeks because they are then too young to leave their parents.)

A baby's age can be assessed in several ways, one of which, the cere color, just discussed. All babies have light ceres. Their eyes appear larger than older birds'. This is because the iris of the eye and the pupil are both solid black. When the bird is about three months old the iris begins to lighten, and by the time the bird is six months old, it has become gray. The pupil, however, remains dark for life.

The baby's beak is black too until it is six or seven

weeks old; then this black begins to fade.

The easiest way of all to identify a young bird is by the striations or shell-like stripes which cover its neck and head. When the bird is between ten and twelve weeks old these stripes begin to slowly disappear and the "cap" becomes white on the various blue-hued birds or a beautiful yellow on the green and yellow birds.

So then, to be sure of getting a young bird, look for a para-

able than a blue one. So choose the shade that appeals to you. You will undoubtedly have to pay more for what are called the "rares"–-opalines, lutinos, albinos, etc.–-and less for the others–-cobalts, mauves, skyblues and yellows. But under the feath-

This is a pair. The male has the blue cere; the female has the brown cere. They may scream and threaten each other but they rarely do any serious damage during these domestic feuds.

keet between six weeks and three months old, with some black on the beak, solid black eyes and shell stripes on its forehead.

WHAT COLOR?

No color is better than another. There is no known relationship between color and intelligence; a green parakeet is not more tame-

ers they are all the same, except for the albinos which have poorer vision.

Nor is there such a thing as a "strain of talkers" to be distinguished by color. Just select a bird that is brightly and fully feathered, with a natural sheen.

HOW ACTIVE?

There are no secrets about discovering a

Irregularly colored birds like these two youngsters may be difficult to judge health wise because of the weird pattern on their plumage. If they are alert, with clear eyes, like these two, it is probably safe to buy them.

parakeet's state of health. His eyes will be clear, his plumage glossy •and full unless he's in molt. Choose a young bird that hasn't lost those color-bars on his head. Choose a lively bird who sits alertly, proudly even, and who reacts to your movements. Avoid one that rests on its "elbows," lacks the long tail, and seems dull and unresponsive.

Do not choose a bird that cannot fly. However, many birds have had the feathers in one wing clipped to restrict flying. These will grow back. And do not clip them again. A bird who tries to fly, only to discover that he can't, quickly becomes timid and unsure of himself and turns into a poor pet.

You will not, of course, accept any bird with a hunched back, swellings, missing toes, ragged feathers, scaly feet, a deformed beak or legs, or watery eyes. Pay attention to the feathers around the vent. If they are missing or badly stained, a bowel disorder is indicated.

If you're wondering what that aluminum band is doing on the parakeet's leg--well, it's a breeder's band. Not all fine parakeets carry a band; often the unbanded bird is just as good.

Today, good parakeets can be purchased at all kinds of stores that sell pets. Their demand has proven so universal that almost all pet shops keep a good and varied supply of parakeets on hand. We also believe that of all the pets you can obtain for your home, a parakeet offers the most in terms of pleasure and enjoyment for the smallest possible cost.

20

Care and Housing

This young budgie is a very poor quality budgie in terms of its being measured against the Budgerigar Standards, but as a pet it might be marvelous.

Which comes first, the parakeet or the cage? The cage. It should be waiting, set up, all in order, when you bring your new pet home in that small cardboard or plastic container the pet dealer provides. Your parakeet's home within your home will be his castle, his retreat from your mad world. So when you choose a permanent cage for him, make sure it's large enough to give him plenty of exercise. Place it in a spot away from direct sun. Make sure it is not in a draft. Put it up high on a cage stand or wall bracket; that way your parakeet can get a bird's eye view of his

An ideal cage for a budgie.

surroundings. A cage cover at night will give him a sense of privacy and security, and help him to doze off quickly.

Cages come in all sizes, styles and prices. You'd be amazed how little--or how much--they can cost. You set the limit.

Almost any metal cage is suitable for a parakeet, provided the bars are not too far apart. Don't spend your money on a fancy, ornamental cage with all manner of gingerbread decorations. Your bird's comfort is what you must consider, not the ornate appearance. Such cages are pretty to look at but are hard to keep clean, and your pet's health should be paramount in all your planning. He'll need plenty of flight room, conveniently placed perches and swings, an easy way to get at food and water, etc.

The Preferred Cage

There are a number of cages on the market designed especially for parakeets-- their bars are horizontal rather than vertical, making it easier for the bird to climb.

Let me repeat: the cage should be large enough so that the bird is not cramped. Otherwise, its tail feathers will constantly be brushing against the sides, and sticking out between the bars; they will be quickly frayed, leaving a dirty, bedraggled bird. This is especially true if the bird is to be permanently confined, and not allowed to fly around the room.

Cages are usually made of metal although some of the more ornamental ones are of wood, bamboo, or woven wicker. These last, while pretty to look at, are impractical for parakeets,

who love to gnaw. A wooden or wicker cage will soon be a terrible sight to behold; more so if it was once painted. Wood also develops cracks and crevices in which pests can hide.

Metal cages may be either stainless steel or chromium-, zinc-, brass- or electro-plated. Stainless steel is the better but more expensive choice. All are easy to clean and will give years of service. But if the metal is cheaply painted, the birds will soon chip

The best cages are found in pet shops.

Irregularly shaped perches are best since they allow the budgie to exercise its grip.

Budgies must have special cages. The wires should be horizontal so the birds can climb and they must be close enough together so the budgie cannot slip its head between them. A budgie's head appears a lot larger than it really is.

it off. If you do choose a painted metal cage, be sure that the paint is baked on. Such a cage is also easier to keep clean and disinfected.

Check any new cage to make sure that no jagged-end wire is protruding. Clip it off or bend it in such a way that the bird cannot injure itself or catch its leg in a loop.

sure the cage is thoroughly dry before the bird is put into it.

Another thing to check is the cage bars. They should be no more than one-half inch apart because a parakeet can easily

Check it too for any paint globs that may have been left in corners; scrape them off with steel wool.

All new cages should be thoroughly washed with hot water and strong detergent to remove any traces of the acid wash they are given at the factory. But be

force his head through a larger opening, and possibly strangle.

The cage bottom should slide in and out like a drawer. This is the easiest type to keep clean.

There should be a two-inch seed guard all around the bottom to keep seed hulls, grit, food, debris and feathers off the floor. Some cages come equipped with them; if yours does not, attachable plastic seed guards are available.

The cage door should be large enough for the parakeet to hop through easily, and it should have a double catch––one to fasten it open, one to fasten it closed securely so that the bird cannot open it with his beak.

The door of the cage should be removable or so hinged that it will stand open when the bird is out of the cage, allowing him to return whenever he chooses. Some cages have a landing perch just outside the door to make entrance easier. If you can't afford a large cage, or if you want an extra flight cage for your pet, a fairly satisfactory one can be constructed from a large wooden box, the larger the better, but at least two feet long and nine inches deep. Fit it with a hinged cover made of a picture-frame covered with one-half inch wire mesh, making sure that no jagged ends of mesh protrude. Stand the box on its narrow end (for cage purposes its length becomes its height), drill holes on either side in

which to fit two or more perches and attachments for seed and water cups, and hang a swing from the top. Paint the inside with a non-toxic white enamel (the paint prepared especially for baby furniture) and the outside any color you prefer. Fit a metal tray into the bottom to make cleaning easier or fashion a tray of aluminum foil.

If you buy a second-hand

Cages like this are not very satisfactory for budgies because they cannot climb on the vertical wires. The cage is also too narrow for the bird to exercise its wings. This kind of cage is suitable for small finches.

cage, or find an old one in the attic, scrub and disinfect it thoroughly, preferably by boiling it in water with a strong disinfectant. If you should then decide to paint it (or to paint a new cage to match your color scheme) be sure to use non-toxic enamel. Apply the paint evenly, making sure there are no hardened globules when the paint dries. Never place a bird in a newly painted cage. Keep him in a temporary cage until you are absolutely sure that the paint is completely dry and odorless. The latex-base paints are always safest.

The cage should have a big hook or eye on its top so that it can be hung from a bracket, floor-stand, or from the ceiling, safe from other pets and mice.

The cage's location should be carefully considered. Parakeets cannot tolerate drafts, and with a cage with bars on all sides the only way to prevent them is to choose a corner of a room that is draft-proof. Nor should the cage be hung in direct sunlight. If you do keep it near a window be doubly sure that along with the sunny area there is a constantly shaded area into which the bird can move.

You'll probably want to keep your bird in a room where there is a lot of family activity, and that is good. But avoid the kitchen unless it is a very large one. The constant fluctuation of temperature due to cooking is bad for the bird; so is gas, if you use that for cooking. Running hot water, pots boiling on the stove, and electrical appliances can also be a source of danger when your bird is out of its cage.

While you may change the location later, it's wise to keep the cage in one spot until the bird becomes used to it. The less often the cage is moved, the easier it will always be for your pet to find his way "home."

Budgies are very sociable animals and they like company whether it be another budgie or a human being. The mutual preening is really a sign of affection, not necessarily sexual affection.

the outside type, the bird must put his head through an opening in the bars to eat. At first he may not realize these cups are there, so you should scatter seed on the cage floor until you know he has discovered them.

Always watch for the accumulation of husks in the seed dish. There is no nourishment in these, so they must be discarded daily. Seed and water cups should be rinsed out once a day and thoroughly washed in suds and rinsed in scalding water weekly.

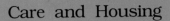

Hanging seed bells are one of the parakeet's favorite snacks.

Get into the habit of changing the seed daily and washing out the seed cups every day; once a week these cups should be sterilized in boiling water.

Seed Cups

Basic furniture consists of perches, seed and water cups, and one or two special treat cups. All cups should be kept full. Parakeets never eat a good square meal; they prefer to nibble all day long.

Newly purchased cages usually come equipped with seed cups. They are attached either to the inside or the outside of the cage. With

Perches

Each cage should be fitted with at least three

This is a show quality opaline cobalt blue hen. She and most budgies prefer to rest on a perch than on a flat surface. Their feet are designed for grasping and not for standing.

perches. Don't have them all of the same diameter. Different-sized rounds help to rest and exercise the feet. One should be placed so the bird can stand on it within comfortable reach of his food and drink cups. Hardwood twigs can be substituted for perches occasion- ally.

Parakeets enjoy chewing the bark. Most birds also enjoy a swing.

It is a good idea to have an extra set of perches to substitute for those that are being cleaned. Perches should never be washed. Washing softens the wood, making it easier to splinter. And if a bird is permitted

to stand for any length of time on a damp perch, he will become rheumatic. Commercial perch scrapers are available; or you can use coarse sandpaper.

Gravel

As we pointed out when discussing cage purchase, the bottom should be equipped with a removable drawer or tray to make cleaning easy. This tray should be covered with a layer of gravel, the commercially prepared kind for parakeets. This gravel (also called "grit") should be discarded weekly when the tray is scrubbed.

And what's the gravel for, you ask? The budgie eats it. Well, not to digest, but to keep in his gizzard to grind the food as it passes through. Remember, birds don't have teeth to use for the chewing and grinding of food; gravel has to do the job. Always be sure there's a layer of the stuff on the bottom of the cage. Not only is it essential for his digestion, it's also great fun to

Gravel paper around the perch would help this beautiful Australian pied cobalt keep its nails trimmed. Notice how long and sharp they are.

Gravel paper on the bottom of the cage and on the perches is necessary. Gravel is also necessary for the budgie's diet.

29

Cuttlebone

You must always keep a piece of cuttlebone attached to the side of the cage. It will help to keep your pet's beak in good condition, and it will serve as a needed diet supplement—it contains calcium and other needed mineral salts. Fasten the cuttlebone securely to the cage with the soft side facing in, close to a perch. Replace it when the soft part has been chewed away.

Bathtubs

They can add to the parakeet's comfort in hot weather. Some birds like to take baths, some don't. If yours is one of the latter, don't force the issue. Instead, try putting seeds in the

Cuttlebone is essential for a budgie's health. These bones easily attach to the cage.

If your budgie is constantly preening itself, you should suspect that it needs a bath.

scratch around in it.

About once every two weeks, the entire cage should be scrubbed and disinfected. But always make sure that the tray and the cage are thoroughly dry before returning the bird to them.

To make it easier, a mat of cedarized or gravel paper—or any ordinary kind of paper—can be placed under the loose gravel to protect the tray.

empty tub until he gets used to jumping in to eat them. Then later surprise him with a little water. Use a bird bathtub, or a small glass bowl with only a little tepid water in the bottom. If your bird avoids the bath placed on the floor of his cage, try the type that can be attached to the door.

It is wiser to give the bird his bath in the morning; then he will be thoroughly dry by nightfall.

Many a parakeet who adamantly refuses to use his tub will fly over to the sink and duck under a dripping faucet. Be careful to see that it's not hot. If he continues to resist the inevitable, there are fine prepared bird sprays on the market. Spray a fine mist over him, and he'll do the rest while preening.

Preening is how your parakeet cleans himself. He runs his feathers through his beak. Periodically, he'll take a bit of oil exuded from a gland at the base of his tail and preen with that. Result: a careful combing. Some say it takes him a week to go through all his feathers—others say it takes only a day. Don't bother to count. Rest assured that preening is perfectly normal.

Budgies must preen themselves in order to stay as clean as these two birds. They like to bathe. Their shiny feathers come from an oil gland at the base of the tail.

A mirror with a treat cup will make any budgie happy.

Toys

"Bird things" can include swings, mirrors, ladders, see-saws, ferris wheels, wagons, roly-polys, bells, whatever. You'll be amazed at all the things you'll think of. After a few weeks your bird will own enough gadgets to fill a shoe box. But don't clutter up your pet's cage with a lot of them. Give him a couple at a time, substitute two more, and alternate them from day to day. Plastic toys are easier to keep clean and less likely to be chewed.

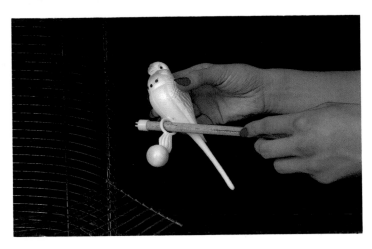

It is amusing to watch a parakeet with a new mirror. Immediately he rushes to greet his new friend. What chuckles and gurgles of delight! Surely the pleasure is contagious. Then cautiously he peeks in back of the mirror and, satisfied that there is no intruder, returns to the image. Perhaps he may try to feed the stranger by regurgitating a little food. This is perfectly normal.

Cage Covers

There are two schools of thought on this, but the consensus is that if you start out using a cover then you must continue the practice. If your house temperature drops suddenly at night, it is wise to use a cover. If the bird is kept in a room where there are lights and TV at night, or street lights and passing cars are visible through a window, a cover will be needed in

Budgies like swings as it reminds them of light branches in their natural habitat.

Budgies must have their toenails filed or clipped.

order for the bird to get its needed sleep.

If you're covering for warmth, use a heavy cover; if for darkness, any opaque fabric will do. Commercially made cage covers are, of course, available.

Grooming

There are two things you may have to do for your bird: trim his toenails and his beak. Caged birds quickly develop over-long

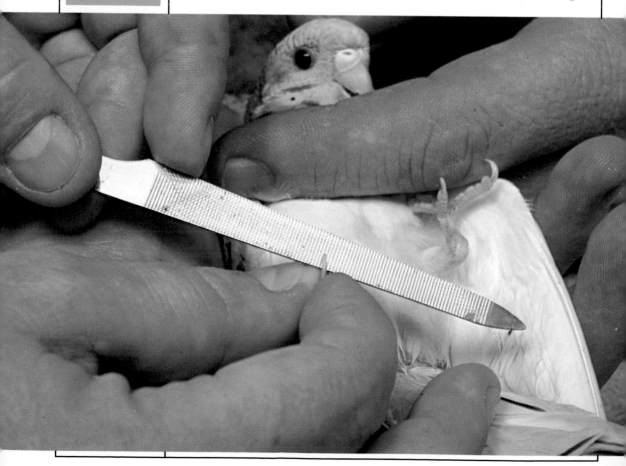

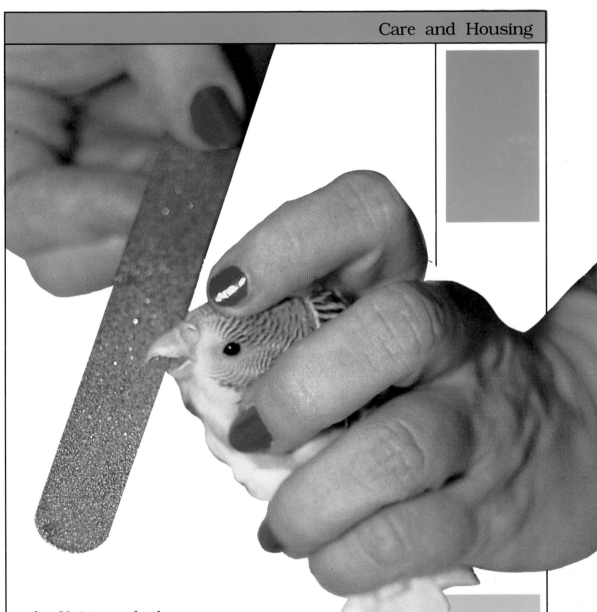

nails. Untrimmed, they curve back in such a way that the parakeet cannot grip his perch. Use nail clippers to snip off the tips. Avoid the dark blood vessel running down the inside; clip short of this. If there is some bleeding, watch carefully; a styptic powder may be used to stop it. After the trimming, your bird will be much more spirited.

If your pet develops a misshapen or overgrown beak it will have to be trimmed back to its normal shape. If you are hesitant to attempt it, engage professional assistance. Use sharp straight nail clippers. Trimming will not hurt the bird, provided it is done before the problem becomes serious.

Budgies that don't get enough calcium to chew on require their beaks to be trimmed by filing, as shown here. The budgie's bill should not be this sharp and pointed.

Clipping your budgie's wings is done by cutting all or most of the long flight feathers on one or both wings. This disables the budgie from flying. The last four feathers should be left on the wing for appearance's sake.

Wing Clipping

This should not be done unless there is a real danger of your bird escaping or hurting himself. Sometimes in summer, with the constant opening and closing of screen doors, it is necessary to restrict the bird's flight. Only the inner feathers need to be trimmed. Leave the last four long feathers on the end of each wing uncut to keep the bird's appearance attractive. Both sides should be clipped evenly.

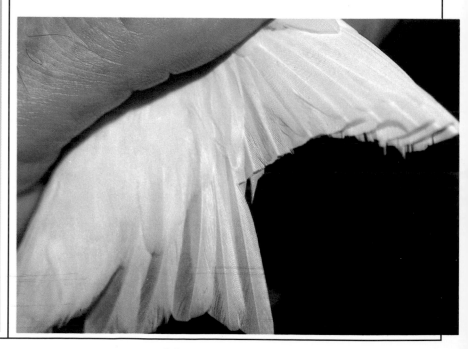

Feeding

One of the joys of keeping a parakeet is the ease with which he can be fed. His basic diet is a seed mix supplemented with vegetable greens and a vitamin supplement.

Buy seed prepared for parakeets/budgerigars only. This is a different mixture from that prepared for canaries. Keep it fresh. Buy in small quantities. The large economy size isn't a bargain if the seed goes stale before you've used it all. The commercially available brands are packed to keep their contents fresh and clean. The ideal parakeet seed contains a mixture of canary and millet seed, plus small amounts of other seeds such as oats and hemp.

As your parakeet eats, he'll crack the seed, swallow the kernel and drop the husk--usually right back in his seed cup. Because of this, his cup may look full of seed when it is only filled with empty husks. Dump them out and refill the cup daily. Do the same with his water; empty out the old, wash the cup, and refill daily. The seed cup should be kept constantly filled. Never let it become empty; a bird deprived of seed for more than 24 hours will dic. There have been many instances of keets starving to death because their owners thought the cups were still full of uneaten seeds.

Millet grains should be large, smooth in consistency and creamy white or light yellow.

Budgies seem to eat a lot but they do not, so buy the best seed possible. Pet shops sell the most fresh seed. To test whether a seed is fresh, merely plant some. Fresh seed sprouts and budgies love to eat the sprouts.

Canary seed should be shiny, plump and smooth. Small quantities of groats (hulled oats) and brown rice make good supplements. Oats (unhulled) should not be fed because the seeds are too hard to crack. While oats are fattening, baby birds need them, especially in cold weather, to maintain their body heat. Most parakeets consider groats great treats—-like candy—-so feed them accordingly.

It is a good idea, when you introduce your young parakeet to his new cage, to strew some seed on its floor. Many youngsters aren't aware that there's a whole seed-cup full of food waiting for them. Until they discover it, it's best to be sure they're eating by sprinkling their seed where they're bound to notice it.

Spice your parakeet's diet with small quantities of varied treat and supplemental foods placed in the treat cup. They'll stimulate his appetite and provide him with the required amounts of many needed minerals and vitamins. Many of these foods are commercially packed in jars. Fill his treat cups daily.

Millet seed in spray form provides him with a source of food similar to what he'd

This red-eyed lutino is being introduced to broccoli. Budgies usually love all kinds of fresh vegetables.

Many owners choose to feed the greens by hand, making this part of their pet's taming and training. Others attach the greens to the side of the cage with a paper clip, removing them after an hour and throwing them away. Never allow greens to remain on the floor of the cage to become gritty and soiled. All greens and fruits should be thoroughly washed in lukewarm water to remove every possible trace of pesticide which, even in a small lingering quantity, can prove fatal. Among the greens parakeets love are: clover, beet tops, grated carrot, alfalfa, celery tops, celery stalks, dandelions,

find back in nature. It's great sport for him to peck away at a spray hung from the cage.

Greens give your budgie his bright eyes and sleek appearance. They should be fed every other day, giving the bird only what he will eat at one "sitting." always removing any left-overs. After a few feedings you will be able to closely estimatc thc quantity. Most birds love greens. Because of this there is always the danger of their dining not wisely, but too well on them, with resultant diarrhea. If this happens, discontinue greens for about a week.

Pet shops sell holders for fresh greens. Budgies should not have fresh greens daily. Watch their droppings. If they become loose, stop the green for a few days.

Keep your eye on your bird's weight and girth. Budgies, like humans and dogs, can overeat if they do not have enough exercise to burn off their excess fat.

The newly acquired parakeet will have enough stress just becoming accustomed to his new environment. Just offer him normal parakeet seed.

Once the bird is acclimated to his new home, you can begin introducing him to some toys.

carrot tops, corn on the cob, chickweed, apple peel.

All should, of course, be freshly cut and washed thoroughly. Most parakeets also love lettuce and parsley. However, these should be fed sparingly since, for most birds, they have a strong laxative effect. Sometimes too, these two favorites "spoil" the birds for other greens which are even more nutritious.

Do not feed a newly purchased budgie greens during his first week with you. And if he has not been fed greens for some time, go easy on them.

Pots of live growing greens are available in pet shops, designed to fit the parakeet's cage. You merely add water and when the greens are about an inch high insert the unit in its holder. This is one way to be absolutely sure the greens are fresh. They do not, of course, take the place of all other greens. Variety is important.

You will also find at your favorite pet counter egg yolk wafers. Since they need no refrigeration this is probably the most convenient method of supplying egg yolks to your bird. In nature parakeets are nomadic and migratory. They drift from placc to place following the seasons. As these flocks of budgies wander

This is a champion gray cock with dirty feet and unruly feathers. He was transported for this photo in a small cardboard carrier and had to walk in his own droppings.

A pair of healthy budgerigars which were only fed budgie seed purchased at the local petshop.

Fresh millet spray is a favorite for budgerigars... both in your home and in Australia, their natural range.

they are constantly exposed to different types of food. Beggars can't be choosers; this is true of parakeets and people. So our little feathered friend must eat what he finds--different foods at different times and places. In our cage at home he must of course have his basic seed diet daily. However, varying the treats and supplements frequently will add a more natural touch and increase his pleasure.

Contrary to popular belief an animal, your parakeet included, cannot select, from a variety set before him, ingredients in the proper proportion to balance his diet. Like children, they have uncontrolled taste preferences. Given a choice between candy and basic food the child will always fill up on sweets and so will a budgie. Therefore it is wise to follow the manufacturer's feeding directions carefully and avoid possible future troubles.

The New Arrival

You will, of course, bring your new pet home in a traveling cage well protected from drafts. When you get him there his new cage should be ready and waiting, prepared according to the instructions given above. Now I have a suggestion to make that you may not want to follow. Leave the new arrival in his cage for at least two weeks. Make no attempt to take him out or to permit him to fly around the house. This does not mean that you cannot begin his hand-taming a day or two after his arrival, but do it in the cage. Let him become adjusted to his new quarters and to feel safe and secure in them. It

Budgies rarely become frlendly and tame immediately. They need training...and the training should start a day or two after the budgie has arrived home.

is highly important that the cage become firmly established in his mind as his "castle" and sanctuary.

You'll of course want to keep him in a spot where there is a lot of family

This champion bird has large, round throat marks which are so desirable. It is also clean and neat...but not young. Birds like this are more difficult to tame and train than a young bird.

activity (although not the kitchen), you will talk to him soothingly on every occasion, calling him by name, and you will see that his cage is kept scrupulously clean and that he is well and properly fed.

Make sure that your new pet starts to eat. He will probably be "off his feed" for a day or

will not be able to resist nibbling at the handy seed. If a bird does refuse to eat, it is a good idea to remove all the perches from the cage so he will be forced to sit on the floor among the seeds.

It is not a good idea, however, to put water on the floor of the cage because the youngster will hop in it, spill it, get his feet wet and perhaps catch his death of cold.

If your young parakeet has difficulty cracking seeds when he is on his own for the first time, help

so because of the strangeness of his situation. Have his seed cup full, but also spread some seed on the floor of the cage. Many young parakeets will huddle on the cage floor the first few days but they

These new birds got their toes caught under the ladder hanging from their perch. Such *traps* should be removed until the birds are fully acclimated.

Introduce feed, water and toys one at a time so the young bird can learn where everything is and what it means.

Be careful when introducing a well established bird with a new arrival as some budgies are very territorial, especially when both birds are males.

him by cracking them in advance. It is rarely necessary to do this for more than the first few days. When the black on a baby's beak fades, he is fully capable of cracking his own seeds.

It is not wise to give a new bird greens immediately. Wait a few days at least, until he becomes better adjusted. If he then refuses them, dip them in water before feeding and, at the same time, remove the water cup. He must learn to like greens; his system needs the nutritional elements they furnish. At the same time, moist greens hanging in the cage will serve as a

substitute for water.

For the first few nights see that the bird gets to bed early. Cover his cage or remove him to a darkened room as soon as he shows signs of drowsiness: his feathers will begin to fluff up and he will become inactive.

On the second day after his arrival you can begin the hand-taming which we will now discuss.

Taming, Tricks, and Talking

Getting your birds to be this well tamed and trained takes effort on your part. It is only a question of patience.

This lutino female budgie is paying serious attention to its lessons. You can tell when a bird is paying attention or when they are distracted.

As we've said, parakeets are bright birds.

They can learn to do many things no matter what their color or age. It's all a matter of personalities—his and yours—and patience. Because parakeets are affectionate birds, they quickly sense friendship. Therefore, gain your bird's confidence before attempting any lessons. Once he enjoys your company, teaching will be fun.

You can start finger-taming your new pet the day after you bring him home. This does not mean that he should be taken out of his cage. It is wiser to keep him caged for about two weeks so that he will become completely adjusted to his new home and regard it as a place of security. But hand-taming should begin immediately because your bird will be seeking new companionship now that he has been separated from his cage mates.

Some feel you should give your parakeet longer—a couple of days, say—to make himself at home.

Talk to him gently, see that he has plenty of food, and keep his cage clean. Just by watching you perform your daily chores he'll get to know and accept you. Keep your move-

ments around his cage at a minimum. Avoid startling him.

After a few days pass a perch or thin wood stick into his cage slowly, speaking softly. Turn it crosswise to his body and press it gently against him where the legs are joined to the body. Repeat this several times. Soon, though most likely not on the first day,

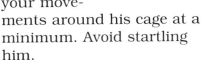

he'll step on the stick. You've gained point one. Now, once he's accustomed to the perch, substitute your finger in the same gentle but deliberate manner. Repeat. After a time he won't be frightened by the presence of your hand. Once he accepts your hand you can gently stroke his chest and head if he'll permit it.

Training a budgerigar to perch on a stick is, perhaps, the easiest of lessons. Merely slowly move the perch towards the budgie and nudge him on the top of his legs (below). He will quickly jump onto the perch. Then you can pick him up on the perch (above) and talk to him in your usual calm manner.

(Some believe in starting first with a T-stick. This consists of two half-inch dowels joined together in the form of the letter *T*, the handle about two feet long, the cross a few inches wide.)

If he flutters wildly whenever you approach him, do not move away. He will think that he has driven you off, and that is bad psychology. If he flutters, or crouches and cries for help, do not be alarmed. Stand there and talk to him soothingly, repeating his name over and over and telling him what a pretty bird he is. What you say isn't important--repeat the alphabet rhythmically if you can think of nothing else--how you say it, is. Your voice should always be gently reassuring.

Never jerk your hand away if the bird flutters. Keep it in the cage until he quiets down, talking gently all the while, and then make another attempt. He will soon come to realize that you mean no harm. Before you know it, he'll be on your finger! Be prepared to reward him with his favorite treat when he takes his first step.

Taming periods should last ten or fifteen minutes, several times a day. End a period with the bird sitting on your finger; never when he flutters away, or cries. Stroke him before withdrawing.

Only after your bird accepts your finger should he be taken out of the cage. Bring him out perched on

One of the very beginning lessons in training your budgie is to get him to perch on your finger. Just keep trying...every young bird can easily be tamed and trained to finger perch.

finger, don't make any startled movements. Remain frozen until he alights. Then go to him with extended finger and return him to the cage. If he refuses, pick him up gently. If he flutters away again, don't chase after him, noisily moving furniture. Wait until he lights and try again. If he lights on a high place like the top of a door or a curtain rod, use the T-stick. If he continues to avoid you, have someone

your finger. In this way he'll associate the finger with entering and leaving the cage, and you'll have a better chance of returning him when you so desire. For the first venture out, wait until after dark. Then he won't try to fly through a closed window if he becomes startled. Fasten open the door of the cage. Get him to perch on your finger and slowly bring him out of the cage. Walk around the room talking to him soothingly for a few minutes and return him to his cage, closing the door. Repeat this several times; at night at first, and then during the day.

If the bird flies off your

A mirror is a budgie's favorite toy. You can use the toy as a decoy to get the budgie to where you want to work with him outside the cage.

You can tell this is a tame bird just by looking at him.

Perches at different heights and thicknesses are advantageous in training and keeping your budgie's feet in good condition.

A skinny perch like this one is not suitable for a budgie unless additional perches are available of varying thickness.

turn out the lights. He will not attempt to fly in the dark. Pick him up gently and return him to the cage. In the daytime a light piece of cloth can be dropped over him to assist in the retrieval.

If there's any chance of his flying into the kitchen, make sure there is nothing hot on which he might perch. His first efforts are likely to exhaust him. After all, the chances are he's never been free to fly before. Once tired, he

can probably be caught in your hand. If he perches out of your reach, gently move him off with your training stick. Eventually he will either let you catch him, perch on your finger, or return to the cage of his own volition if he can find the door. For this reason it's a good idea to have a

landing strip just outside the cage door.

The correct way to hold a bird is in the palm of the hand, with the thumb and first finger forming a circle around its neck, and the little finger around its tail. The second and third finger confine the body and legs. Hold the bird in this manner and scratch its head until it relaxes. Remember

that keets enjoy having their heads and throats stroked, so do this constantly during all its taming and training.

When he'll stay on your finger as you walk him around, hold your hand to your shoulder and try to get him to move on to it. A bit of his favorite treat

52

placed there sometimes helps. Before long you will discover that your shoulder has become his favorite resting spot–either that or the top of your head; or the frame of your eyeglasses if you wear them.

Be patient. Be kind. You're on the road to further training because now you've tamed your parakeet.

HOUSE RULES

Make it a rule not to let your bird out of his cage until you've made sure that no dangers exist. Winds and drafts can slam doors. Pilot lights on stoves can singe feathers. Large mirrors or windows can create illusions of open space for him to smack into. An open window or a hole in a screen is bound to be explored, inside and out. Running water in a shower or faucet will attract

and scald him if the water happens to be hot. Vacuum cleaners, air conditioners, fans, mixers, and toasters can all be dangerous weapons if your parakeet has the run of the house while they are being used.

TRICKS

The scope of your parakeet's repertoire can range from beak tricks to feet tricks to acrobatics! You'll be constantly amazed at what he can do. Often you have only to provide the gadget, and he'll provide the trick himself. Every toy you buy will afford him hours of fun. He'll even practice his act when he's alone!

For some people, however–but not for parakeets–teaching tricks can be a tedious job, particularly if the bird's wings haven't been clipped to prevent his flying away when he gets bored. Some people prefer to keep the wings unclipped and the bird's beauty intact–and let the birds devise their own tricks, which

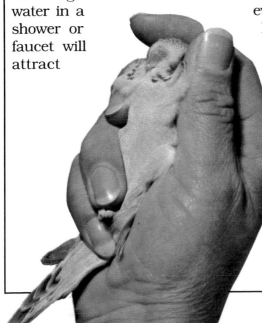

The photo above shows the WRONG WAY to hold your budgerigar. The photo below shows the CORRECT WAY to hold your budgie.

If your budgie loves millet sprays as much as most budgies, you can use this to tease him up the steps of a ladder. Once your budgie learns this trick he'll expect to be rewarded every time he performs it.

they always do if given half a chance.

For this purpose play-pens are available in pet shops. These are wooden, plastic or metal trays equipped with toy ladders, crossbars, bells, etc. They differ in price according to the elaborateness of their devices. After studying one, perhaps you would rather assemble your own. Remember, however, that strings, wires, loops and holes are dangerous, so build your gymnasium with that thought in mind.

However, if you wish a more active role, here goes:

All tricks are variations of three basic acts: riding, climbing, and using his beak. Teach him this basic repertoire and he'll be a circus by himself. Three things make up a trick: using one of basic instincts (his), guidance (yours) and perseverance (yours). Parakeets love to clamber, push, butt their heads and pull. If you want him to pull something, first put the string in his beak. Later he'll pick it up himself. If you want him to ride, set him in the car and guide him with a gentle prod to the tail.

Riding: Perch your parakeet on your finger and bring him to the object you want him to ride and encourage him to hop off onto the car. Repeat several times. Try again the next day. After a short time he'll start hopping on all by himself.

Climbing: Parakeets love to clamber up and down the sides of their cage. A ladder is easy for them— the rungs are horizontal perches. Set the ladder at an angle and place your bird on the bottom rung. He might move up by himself. Otherwise, gently give him an encouraging prod. He'll conquer the first rung or two. Again, another gentle nudge, another rung conquered. Repeat this bottom-to-top business until he goes up by himself consistently without your help. Then teach him to go down in the same manner. However, to give him confidence, hold your hand about him loosely as

you nudge him down to the lower rung. Once he masters this he'll be climbing up and down as if it were the world's easiest sport.

Using the beak: For pulling toys, place the object in his beak. Then, while holding him, show him what he is to do—pull! You may have to press a bit until he opens his beak. But open it he will, so don't use force. Once he knows how to hold he can quickly learn to carry things.

In pushing tricks, such as rolling a ball, place his beak against a ball and

It is not too difficult to teach your budgerigar to use his beak for pulling.

walk him forward. This is something he may learn to do by himself--just provide the ball.

Bells, mirrors, and other props bring a quick response if you'll just demonstrate what can be done with them—and sometimes even if you don't. Leave a few items in his cage and let him practice when he's in the mood.

TALKING

There are many different beliefs concerning talking parakeets. Yet when you brush the little variations aside, almost everyone agrees that any parakeet will learn to talk, given half a chance.

Your bird will learn nothing until he has been treated with kindness and feels perfectly at ease with you. Its attachment to you and the sound of your voice are very important. That is why the person who is most attached to the bird should undertake its formal training. Others can help by constantly repeating the word or phrase the bird is supposed to learn, trying to use the same intonation, but that is all. Never let another person try to teach a new word while you are still working on another one. It cannot be emphasized too strongly that the personality of the trainer plays the most important part in teaching a bird to talk. It is *you,* and not the words you say, that has meaning for your parakeet; the words are just pleasant noises that he associates with you.

Any parakeet can learn to talk. Sex makes

It is possible to almost guarantee that every budgie can talk if properly trained.

old.

According to parakeet expert Milton North: "To start your bird on the way to a good vocabulary, pick out one word—just one word that you wish to start with. Use something simple, like `hello' or `baby,' and do not go any further until this word has been mastered. Place your pet on your finger and speak very clearly, a little louder than your normal conversational voice. Repeat this one word several

no difference; it's a mistaken idea that males are better talkers. A parakeet will learn quicker if he's alone than if he has company; it's possible, but difficult, to train two (they distract each other). A youngster will learn quicker than an older bird; progress will be more rapid with a bird less than six months

A parakeet will learn more quickly if kept in isolation from other birds.

Don't try to train your budgie to do a trick and at the same time try to teach him to speak. The budgie can only concentrate on one trick at a time.

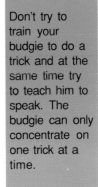

For some strange reason if you put a parakeet who speaks in with a parakeet who doesn't speak, the speaker often returns to the normal parakeet chatter and does not teach the other bird how to talk. Often, they forget to talk at all and get involved (lower photo) in more serious endeavors.

times. Then, bring your budgie closer to your mouth—let him see your lips as you pronounce this word, and say it over and over again. After about fif-

teen minutes, place your pet back in his cage."

Once your parakeet has gained full control and mastery of this one word, then and only then go on to another. You can go on to a short phrase employing the word he's just learned. Preface new lessons with a run-through of the old. You may find that he adds the new word to the old without your coaching!

Others feel that it is probably best to start out by teaching the bird its name, or a short rhythmic

phrase that includes its name—nothing so inane as "Polly wants a cracker," but something along that line. Use a little imagination. It is not a bad idea to make the first phrase answer the usual questions that visitors commonly ask the bird, answers such as "I'm okay," or "Fine, how are you?" or "My name is Budgie—what's yours?"

Rhythmic phrases are probably better than one or two short words. They may take a little longer to learn at first, but the next phrase will come that

much easier. Also, if he slurs only one word of a phrase, it's easy for you or your guests to recognize—or admit—that the bird is indeed saying something. If he slurs the only word of a one-word phrase, those doubting friends of

What could be more enjoyable than a finger-trained budgie that speaks your language!

These very young birds are ideal to train and tame, but they are a bit young for voice training as their vocal apparatus may not be fully developed.

yours hear nothing but noise.

Repeat the word over and over each time you go near the cage, or when the bird is on your finger or your shoulder. Some authorities believe that it is easier to teach a bird to talk if he is kept in his cage with the trainer standing to one side where the bird can hear but not see him. If he sleeps on a lesson, he's quite likely to remember it better, so talk to him after

slipping his cover on at night and before lifting it in the morning.

There are on the market several records to teach parakeets how to talk. Some people record certain phrases on a tape recorder, repeating them over and over. The secret of this method is the sure, clear, slow enunciation and constant repetition. It won't be nearly as boring to your parakeet as it is to you. Once he learns to accept it, he'll be carrying on spirited conversations with your machine.

During the training sessions, outside distractions should be avoided; for example, playing the radio or television at that time must be forbidden. Some people advise covering the cage with a light cloth during these sessions: not his night cover, but a separate piece of linen or muslin. This should be of a solid color, as a pattern might be distracting. Removing his seed cup an hour or so before the lesson also seems to be helpful; if he's slightly hungry he's more alert and more aware of the recording. But be very sure to replace the food immediately afterwards.

Training is a slow job that requires patience. Many trainers have felt like giving up in disgust one day only to go into the bird's room and hear it talking to itself. Once a keet has fifteen or twenty words in his vocabulary, he will start adding new ones fast. Sometimes it takes only a couple of days for a good talker to learn a whole new sentence.

Milton North continues: "The length of time it takes for a parakeet to learn how to talk will vary. A rare `genius' may learn to say his first word after a week or two, and there are some at the other end who may take from nine months to nearly a year before uttering the first word. Don't despair if your budgie doesn't start chattering as quickly as you'd like him to. Budgies are very like humans, and often we find that the slow starters run away with the prizes." How long did it take *you* to utter your first word?

But once a bird has learned to repeat his first few words and phrases, there will be no stopping him. You'll hear him repeating words and phrases he's overheard although they were never addressed to him.

Once a bird has started talking he can be taught progressively

These birds are the proper age for voice training. As you speak to them very gently, observe which of the birds is more attentive. Select the attentive bird for further voice training. Petshops have training records for budgies. It greatly assists you in training your parakeet to speak.

Preparatory to talking, many parakeets puff up their throats like the bird shown here.

Exercise and diet make healthy birds...don't even think about taming or training a sick bird. These two birds are ready for training.

longer sentences. Always teach the entire sentence, not just parts of it. If the bird repeats it badly or slurs some words, don't work on the bad parts; instead repeat the entire sentence emphasizing those words clearly which are distorted or missing. Experiments have shown that the letters *m, n,* and *I* are difficult for the parakeet to pronounce; the letters *p, t* and *k* are easy. So take this into consideration when selecting your phrases.

Training a parakeet to whistle is easier than teaching him to talk. However, this should be delayed because once he learns to whistle he will keep it up incessantly and pay no attention to his speech lessons. Wait until he's learned a few words and sentences before you teach him to

whistle and to sing. To teach him to whistle a tune, whistle only the opening bars at first. When he has mastered them, whistle them over but add the next few bars. Always start from the beginning, and then go on to the new phrase. A budgie can be taught to sing a whole song in this same fashion, but it takes a long time.

Health Care and First Aid

Exercise and diet are the keys. Your parakeet will do his best to keep himself clean, and with proper perches and floor gravel his feet should take care of themselves. However, accidents can happen, illness can strike, so it is wise to be prepared for some of the more common contingencies.

Do not attempt to treat a sick bird beyond these few "home remedy" suggestions. If they do not bring quick results, or if you have any reason to think that your keet may be seriously ill, consult a

It is important to know when a bird is sick. If you have any doubt, remove the sick bird since it may infect its feathered friends.

Budgies like this one, active, alert and fully feathered, may be assumed to be healthy. Remember that pet shops stock a variety of medicaments formulated for budgies and other kinds of birds.

veterinarian at once. You will recognize that your bird is not well from his ruffled feathers, loss of appetite, listlessness, excessive thirst, discharge from eyes and nostrils, watery discolored droppings or perhaps convulsions.

Frequently a sick bird will respond to a simple change of food, a lighter diet, and a long period of rest.

Perhaps the first thing to do when you have a sick bird on your hands is to turn his cage into a "hospital". This assumes, of course, that you have only one bird. If you have two or more, you should isolate the sick bird at once. For this you can use any cage—even a small one—because

his stay there will be only temporary. Cover three sides of it with heavy cloth and keep a lighted, shielded electric bulb close to it to provide added warmth. Try to keep an even temperature of about 85°F. A gentle laxative like milk of magnesia can be administered while you consider further measures. Use a medicine dropper to administer a few drops.

Many ailments will yield to modern antibiotics now available especially for birds. There is a prepared hulled millet seed that provides aureomycin and can be given to the bird in place of his regular daily seed for a period of about fifteen days.

If a bird won't drink or eat, use a medicine dropper to dose him. Give him one drop at a time to make sure he doesn't choke on it, and always make sure that the medication is at the tip of the dropper in order not to force air into him. The bird can also be "force-fed" in this manner with honey diluted in water. About ten drops a day, one at a time, is enough. Put the tip of the dropper into the beak from the side.

INVALID DIET

If the patient will eat, feed him only easily digested foods: groats (hulled

This normal light green budgie is a champion with absolutely magnificent throat markings. Before birds like this are brought to an exhibition, they should be checked by a veterinarian who specializes in birds, to be sure it is not carrying any infectious disease.

oats) or
bread and milk with corn syrup or honey.

RESPIRATORY DISEASES

There are several, but you won't be able to differentiate among them. They affect parakeets with symptoms much like those of the human cold: sneezing, mucus discharge, sinus inflammation, lethargy, shortness of breath and wheezing. "Hospitalize" the bird and give him the antibiotic treatment as described above. Tempt the

Genetics *defects*, like the yellow spot on the back of these budgies' heads, are not infectious but they are transmissible.

bird to eat or feed as described. If antibiotics are not available, give four or five drops of whisky in a tablespoon of milk. If the droppings are loose and watery, see the treatment for diarrhea.

Colds: Colds are generally caused by exposing the bird to a draft. He can withstand cold temperatures, but never a draft. He'll puff up, partially close his eyes, ruffle his feathers and appear listless. A severe cold will even cause his eyes to darken noticeably; this disappears as the cold gets better. Keep your parakeet in warm temperatures of 85 to 90°F, 24 hours a day. Give him tepid, fresh water only. Let him rest in his cage. Bird vitamin tonics are a big help.

Pneumonia: A parakeet with pneumonia will exhibit all the symptoms of a cold as well as wheezing and gasping for breath. Keep him very warm (about 85°F) around-the-clock. Provide the same treatment as for colds.

DIARRHEA

Sometimes this is a simple ailment in itself; at other times it is the symptom of something more serious. He'll be listless, his feathers will ruffle, and he'll soil his vent feathers with loose droppings. The bird's normal droppings are semi-solid, but if they become green and watery, and the feathers around the vent are badly soiled, begin treatment.

Stop feeding all greens and fruit. Hospitalize; keep him warm. Give a couple of drops several times a day of either Kaopectate, Pepto-bismol or milk of bismuth. The drops can be given either by a medicine dropper or by mixing them in with the feed. Commercially prepared oats and groats along with boiled milk will also help straighten him out.

CONSTIPATION

Listlessness along with few, but hard, droppings is the indication. Give him more greens in his diet. A drop or two of mineral oil or milk of magnesia fed with a medicine dropper will also help, or put a pinch or two of Epsom salts into the drinking water. Always be sure the oil is at the tip of the dropper so as not to force air into the bird. Exercise will help too. What can also happen is that the vent gets clogged with a matting of feces and feathers. This can be softened and removed with warm water and a cotton swab.

VOMITING

It is instinctive for keets to regurgitate their food to feed the young. Sometimes they try to feed the "bird friends" they see in mirrors. Do not be concerned unless it becomes frequent or is accompanied by other symptoms. If he throws shelled seed out of his crop and it has a bad smell, try

This budgie looks well but its droppings were very loose. Loose droppings may indicate diarrhea and the bird should be treated.

A budgie peering from the hole in its nest box.

This champion female green budgie may suffer from egg binding whether she has mated or not.

a pinch of Epsom salts in the drinking water.

CROP BINDING

The crop is a small food storage reservoir that holds food until the gizzard is ready for it.

Sometimes it becomes compacted with a solid mass of dry food, string, paper, etc. Mineral oil should be given, and then the crop should be gently kneaded. If this treatment fails, veterinary surgery is called for.

EGG BINDING

This, of course, occurs only in the female that cannot pass her eggs. We discuss it in the section on Breeding.

APOPLEXY

On occasion a bird can appear to be in the best of health when it suddenly falls to the floor of the cage, struggles a little as if it had a broken wing, and dies.

This is often the result of overeating and/or dietary deficiency, particularly lack of vitamin E, which can be supplied in wheat-germ oil.

MOLTING PROBLEMS

Molting is the *natural* process of feather replacement. Old feathers are shed, and new ones grow to take their place. Normally, the molting period is related to the length of the day and seasonal temperature changes. However, your parakeet is subjected to artificial light and differ-

ent tcm perature variations. He's liable to molt at any time, regardless of the sea- son. Make sure he's eating well during the molt. Special molting food will help his new feathers to arrive in glowing color. During a normal molting period new feathers should replace the old at a constant rate. Should your bird show bare patches and/or lose his ability to fly, this is not normal and requires inves- tigation.

French molt: is an un- natural condition in which the bird is *constantly* molt- ing, losing old feathers, growing new ones; at no time does it appear sleek and fully feathered as it should. The quills are soft, pull out easily and are filled with a dark foreign substance. There are several theories, none of which have proven con- clusive, regarding the cause of French molt. Aviarists agree, however, that a liberal variety of supplementary and treat foods (of the latter, egg-yolk wafers espccially) be pro- vided frequently.

FEATHER PICKING
Some birds, like children biting their finger nails, ac- quire the nervous habit of pulling out their own feath- ers and, on occasion, eating them. This should

This albino budgie is suffering from French molt. It constantly pulls out its own feathers.

This bird is a feather chewer and keeps stripping the under feathers from its chest and wing.

not be confused with the bird's normal habit of plucking out loose feathers. Bare spots can be soothed with vaseline. Try keeping the bird in a slightly cooler atmosphere. Give him something to keep him occupied-- more flying time, perhaps.

MITES, FEATHER LICE

The parakeet with his everlasting preening quickly dislodges such pests, but it is up to you to keep the cage clean. Red mites may infect your bird. They hide in crevices or on the cage bottom and come out at night to attack him. If you suspect them, throw a piece of white cloth over the cage and check it the next morning for tiny red spots. If found, attack on two fronts. Kill the parasites on the bird and exterminate them from the cage. Remove him from the cage and apply one of the many good powders that are on the market. Apply the powder directly to the bird's body, especially under the wings, and work it well into the feathers. Mite sprays are also effective and easier to use since they eliminate the necessity of holding the bird. For the cage use one of the mite powders or sprays. Apply kerosene with a small brush to all the places where the pests might be lurking. Clean the cage with boiling water and then disinfect it. Make sure that it is thoroughly dry before returning the bird to it. Replace all perches with new ones. Generally speaking, any of the aerosol sprays designed for the eradication of such pests are satisfactory.

A fairly recent development is the use of long-lasting insect repellents. These are packaged in small plastic and metal containers. The seal is removed and the container hung on the cage. This emits an invisible, odorless insect-repelling vapor for periods of up to three months.

INTERNAL PARASITES

These are rare among caged birds who have never been exposed to sources of infestation. They include roundworms, tapeworms, flukes, and various other parasites. Only a vet can detect and prescribe for them. If you notice anything suspicious in your pet's droppings, take a sample to the vet for microscopic examination.

OIL DUCT OBSTRUCTION

The parakeet preens his feathers with the oil which is secreted by a special gland at the base of his

When feather pluckers are cured...which is very rare...the new feathers are neither the same color nor the same texture.

If your budgie develops sore feet, change the perches to a different thickness. Be sure they are smooth. Then medicate the feet.

SORE FEET

Try to find the cause. It may be the roughness of the perch; if so, replace it immediately. Treat the feet with a daily bath of alcohol diluted with water, and then a zinc oxide ointment.

URINARY TROUBLE

A urinary ailment is indicated if your pet drinks an excessive amount of water and its feces are mostly liquid. Treatment with aureomycin is frequently effective.

BROKEN BONES

If at all possible, wrap a gauze bandage around the body to immobilize the bird and take him to the vet. If you feel competent enough to "do it yourself," follow these instructions.

If the wing is broken, fold the wing into its natural position

tail. Sometimes the nipple of this gland becomes clogged. Massage it gently with a bit of cotton soaked in warm water and then press out the dried material so that the oil can flow again.

with the bone ends touching and wind a one-inch strip of gauze about the body and the other wing, several times, holding it in place with strips of adhesive tape. Leave it on for about three weeks.

If a leg is broken, make a tiny plaster cast. Use surgeon's plaster, available in drug stores, or Johnson's Duo Adhesive. Have an assistant hold the leg outstretched with the bone ends touching. Apply a thin layer of plaster to the leg. As it sets press three half-lengths of flat tooth-picks into it, then add a little more plaster. Now wind a narrow strip of gauze around the mass so that it sticks to the adhesive, and hold the bird in position until the cast sets. Allow it to remain in place for three weeks at least. At the end of that time, remove the cast carefully. Vinegar will help to dissolve the plaster.

POISONING

Fast treatment is important. Give your pet a laxative—about four or five drops of milk of magnesia, drop by drop with a medicine dropper, works well because it is alkaline and an antidote for several acid poisons. Hydrogen peroxide is also good if you don't know what the poison is; dilute it half-and-half in water. If you do know the poison, administer a few drops of its known antidote diluted in water.

Paints, especially those containing lead or linseed oil, are a frequent cause of poisoning. So are rodent poisons and the insecticides left on unwashed vegetables, or sprayed on house plants. After giving your pet first-aid treatment, phone your vet, tell him what you think the poison is, and follow his instructions.

WOUNDS

Clip the feathers around the cut and open it to view.

If your budgie breaks a leg, the vet can easily set it in splints as shown here.

73

Swab it gently with peroxide. If the bleeding is excessive or the cut seems large, take your pet to the vet. Cuts heal in about eight days. Keep your bird warm and comfortable.

BROKEN FEATHERS

There may come a time when you'll want to remove a broken tail or wing feather. Don't hesitate to pull it out. It will come out painlessly with a firm tug. A new feather will begin to grow in. If the quill is not pulled out, a new feather will not grow until the bird molts.

SHOCK

Your bird will lay prostrate on his side on the cage floor. Hold him in your cupped hands to warm his body. A drop or two of warm coffee, strong tea, or whisky can be administered with a medicine dropper, a drop at a time, to act as a stimulant.

SUDDEN CHILLS, HEAT PROSTRATION

A sudden temperature change may give your bird a chill, or an over-heated room with poor ventilation may cause heat prostration. Don't go from one extreme to the other. A chilled bird needs warmth, but not too much; an overheated bird needs to be cooled, but not suddenly. Gently warm the huddling, shivering bird in your hand. Place the overheated bird in an airy (but not drafty) area. Cool drinking water will also help to reduce its temperature.

Broken feathers should be pulled out so a new, healthy feather might grow in its place. The loss of a single feather will not affect the bird's flying ability.

Breeding

As we said in the section on Choosing Your Parakeet, budgies kept as pets, hand-tamed, trained, and allowed out of their cages to play, seldom make good breeders. Usually you are wasting your time if you attempt to breed them.

This is not to say that breeding is difficult. To the contrary, it is a hobby that even a child can carry on without any big expenditure of money; nor does it require a great deal of time. But you must start with a pair of birds that have been chosen for breeding purposes only. Then later, if you wish, the babies can be separated from the parents at an early age, raised in individual cages, hand-tamed while they are very young and sold at premium prices.

The markings on a budgie's forehead are a good indicator of youth. The fully striped forehead indicates a very young bird. Once the bird matures, it loses the stripes on its forehead.

75

The parent birds should be fully mature, one year old or older, and be well nourished although not fat. They should be strong and active. The male's cere should be bright blue, the female's dark tan or brown.

The breeding cage, since there will be two birds living in it, should be as large as possible. As we pointed out in the section on Housing, metal cages are best; however, home-built cages of wood covered with wire mesh can be used if it is important to keep down costs. You cannot, however, econo-mize on the nest box which you will have to add. These are sold in pet shops at varying prices. They are wooden boxes about five inches square and nine to eleven inches high. There is an entrance hole about two inches wide; and the top is hinged to give easy access for observation and cleaning. There is a perch inside the box, the bottom of which is a hollowed-out block of wood, a wooden "nest" whose diameter is about 4 inches and whose depth is about .75 inch. The hollow is essential to keep the eggs from rolling around. The box should be removable for easy clean-ing. No nesting material is required. The female lays her eggs on the bare wood.

This nest box should be either inside the large flight cage, or it should be at-tached to the outside with its opening hole flush with a hole or door in the side of the larger cage. This cage will, of course, be equipped with the necessary accessories and perches described in the section on Housing. It should be placed in a quiet, secluded spot and *left there.* The birds will not breed if they are disturbed except for feeding and sanitation purposes.

Parakeets will mate at any time of the year; they do not have a definite breeding period. In general though, in the north, spring and summer are the best times. In the south, it is too warm in summer; they should be bred during the winter. In the long run, however, the birds will decide for themselves. Not only do they know no season, but they will breed constantly; quite often the female will start laying eggs

This pied male on top of the nest box beckons the opaline female to enter the box and sit on the eggs.

Three-day-old budgie chicks

again before her previous brood has left the nest.

No pair should be allowed to breed more than three times a year, however, as it will weaken them—both the parents and the future offspring. As soon as the young can shift for themselves and have been removed to their individual cages for hand-raising, the nest box should be removed from the cage.

Some parakeets will mate soon after they are placed together in a cage and have discovered the nest box. Others will take a long time. You must wait and let nature take its course. It is fun to watch the male woo and win the female. Sometimes she will reject him violently; if she

injures him it is better to separate the birds and secure either another male or another female.

You will know that the mating has been completed when the female begins to take a great deal of interest in inspecting the nest box, hopping in and out all the time. Soon she will remain inside throughout the day, rejoining her mate outside on a perch at night. Sometimes the male will feed her; sometimes she will come out to feed herself.

A few days after you first notice the trips to the nest, carefully look in. Eggs? Fine! The female will continue laying until there are about five to ten resting in that hollow. The first egg will hatch in about 18 days, and others will follow on alternate days, until the entire clutch has been hatched. This means that there will be babies in all stages of growth in the nest at the same time; some almost fully feathered, others newly hatched and naked (they'll stay that way for about a week).

EGG BINDING

Sometimes an egg sticks in the cloaca and the female cannot pass it or any waste products or urine; toxemia soon sets in. You may not see her straining to pass the egg but you will see her sitting on the bottom of the cage, all ruffled and lethargic. Feel gently on both sides of the cloaca and you will sense the egg—if that is what is causing the trouble. Put her in a perchless cage to make sure she remains on the floor. Keep her warm by placing the cage over some source of steady heat, such as an electric heating pad. A soft cloth on the bottom of the cage will help. If the heat doesn't help, you can try filling a smooth-pointed medicine dropper with mineral oil. Hold the bird carefully but firmly and gently insert the dropper between the cloaca and the egg; move the tip of the dropper around the egg, squeezing out oil as you do so.

If she cannot pass the

An opaline hen with her youngsters in a disposable nest box.

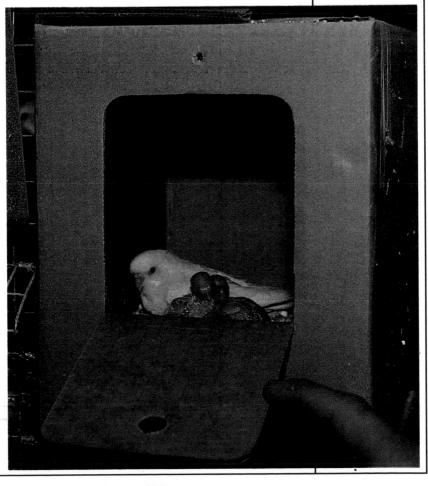

79

Can you find the four budgie babies here? They are three days apart in age.

egg now with the lubrication, there is only one thing to do. Save her life by breaking the egg, letting its contents run out; crush the shell with a pair of tweezers and pull out the pieces. If you find another egg behind the first, wait and see if it can be passed naturally. If not, it will have to be destroyed as well. If the female suffers from egg binding a second time it is probably wise not to attempt to breed her again.

BABY CARE

The baby birds require no special care or feeding on your part. The chicks are fed at first by the mother; when they get older, the father also participates. There is no harm in your opening the lid of the nest box to watch their progress even though the parents will appear to make a great fuss. They should be given fresh greens during this period.

The babies will foul the nest and it will have to be cleaned in spite of the parents' objections. Remove the babies to a temporary bowl and give the hollow block a good scouring with a stiff brush. Do not wash or wet it. Dampness might prove fatal.

As the young become fully feathered they should be taken from the nest--they will be hopping and flitting around by that time and eating on their own--and placed in individual cages if you intend to tame them, or in cages by sex, if you are going to raise them as breeders. Put their food on the floor of the cage for the first week or so, until they get used to eating it out of the feed cup. Their seed mixture should be hulled oats (groats), white millet and canary seed--this

The Australian pied female and her mate, a yellow-face sky blue, and their babies. The oldest is a week old.

Budgerigars maintained in groups under aviary conditions can be varied in color or essentially uniform in color, according to the tastes of their owner. For color-breeding purposes, of course, stricter controls must be applied.

Breeding

These babies are three to eleven days old.

last in about 60% proportion because it is easier to crack.

If the female starts laying a second batch of eggs before all of her young are out of the nest, it is wise to remove them. Many females have been known to kill babies who got in the way while they were laying eggs. Budgies will continue to breed for about ten years; however they are at their best during the first three or four.

Genetics

The ancestors of all parakeets, regardless of present color, were green. Fortunately, you won't have to begin with the green, but you can more or less determine your palette by remembering that green remains the dominant influence in all matings. To understand why parakeets have different colors, and

All budgerigars started from the wild green budgie found today in Australia. The first popular variety was the blue which is nothing more than a green in which all the yellow has been lost.

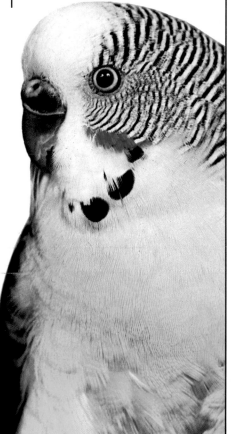

An interesting budgie color is the lemon yellow with a black eye.

how to breed for these particular colors, we must turn to the science of genetics. First explained by the monk Gregor Mendel in 1865, the laws of heredity did not become generally known and accepted until the early 1900s. Genetics is the study of how offspring inherit the features, traits and colors of their parents and grandparents.

It is sometimes difficult for those who have had no training in biology to understand Mendel's laws. But explained in everyday English it is not too difficult, and that is what we will attempt to do now.

The reproductive cell of the female is called an ovum or egg; that of the male, the sperm. When sperm penetrates ovum, a new individual is conceived. Each parent contributes half of its genes. Genes are like tiny packages of coded

information, linked together like a string of beads into what is called a chromosome. Chromosomes are always paired *except* when the ovum or sperm is being formed; then the chromosome pairs split. Half of the mother's genes are in the ovum; half of the father's are in the sperm. The two meet in the impregnated ovum, and a baby is on its way. The newly paired chromosomes contain the detailed blueprints of the baby's heredity--half from one parent, half from the other. But what if these halves differ? A baby can't be both tall and short, blue-eyed and brown-eyed.

Mendel noticed that when he crossed tall garden peas with dwarf peas, the offspring were not medium-sized peas as one would suppose, but *all* were tall. The blueprints (genes) for tall had taken precedence over the genes that specified dwarf: they *dominated* them, and that is how the term "dominant," now commonly used in genetics, originated. The weaker blueprint for size, dwarf, receded into the background--it was *recessive*. It was still there; it just didn't show. It was dominated by its "better half."

This is why many times

hereditary traits *appear* to skip a generation. They are there really; we just don't recognize them. We know this today. But naturalists didn't until Mendel came along.

When he bred that second generation of peas (the ones that looked tall but came from tall and dwarf parents) he found that the new pea vines were *not* all

All of these budgies came from the same parents, but from different matings.

tall, that one out of every four was dwarf. There were still, however, no medium-sized pea vines in this third generation. Just tall or dwarf, nothing in between. When the dwarfs of this third generation were bred together, their offspring were *all* dwarfs. When the talls were bred together,

The parents have unstriped foreheads while the babies have striped foreheads.

however, the expected didn't happen. Some of the talls produced only talls but some produced dwarfs. Mendel worked out the mathematics of it: 25% dwarf, 75% tall; *but*—of that 75%, one-third would be dominantly tall and the other two-thirds (50%) would look tall but they would be carrying the recessive dwarf genes.

Now let us forget about Mendel's peas and see what happens when we apply his findings to parakeets. Let us substitute for the tall pea, the normal green color of the parakeet; and for the dwarf pea, the normal blue colored parakeet. Breeders now know from long experimentation that green is dominant over all other parakeet colors, and that blue is recessive to green. The genes which dictate color in the green bird are dominant; those which dictate the color of the blue budgie are recessive. What happens when these genes meet?

For the purpose of explanation, let us call the dominant color *solid green.* Let us call the combination of dominant green over recessive blue *hybrid green.* Because blue is recessive there can be no such thing as a hybrid blue. We will

call it *pure blue.*

Let us assume that each mating gives birth to eight baby parakeets. There are six possible combinations that can turn up among these eight:

1. If both parents are solid green, the eight children will be solid green.

2. If both parents are pure blue, the eight children will be pure blue.

3. If one parent is solid green and the other pure blue, the eight children will be hybrid green.

4. If both parents are hybrid green, of the eight children there will be two solid green, two pure blue, and four hybrid green.

5. If one parent is solid green and the other hybrid green, of the eight children there will be four solid green and four hybrid green.

The beautiful throat markings on these birds deserve to be preserved by inbreeding these birds together. Inbreed for one characteristic at a time.

Three high quality birds which are suitable for breeding stock. The colors shown are pied light blue, normal light blue and normal cinnamon gray.

6. If one parent is pure blue and the other hybrid green, of the eight children, four will be pure blue and four will be hybrid green.

These averages will not, of course, appear in any one particular mating. They have been derived by counting a great many matings and averaging them. Nor is it possible to tell the solid greens from the hybrid greens--they will all *look* the same. But the solid greens will give birth *only* to solid greens while the hybrid greens will throw *both* types of green as well as blue.

MUTATIONS

All this being true, you may rightfully ask, if each parent passes its hereditary traits on to its offspring with such mathematical precision, how can

This gray winged light green cock is a true champion quality budgie.

there ever be any new colors, sizes, and traits? What about evolution? The answer is that in some way still not known to science the genes for form or color are inexplicably changed in one parent, and then passed on to the children.

Such an unaccounted-for change is called a *mutation*.

A mutation is produced when a gene is so changed that it results in an inheritable trait; a change that breeds true and can be passed on to its children and grandchildren.

HYBRIDIZATION

Do not confuse mutation with hybridization. A hybrid is the offspring of two different species or varieties. An example of hybridization in birds would be the offspring of a canary mated with a wild bird such as a linnet or a goldfinch.

To date we have not discovered any parakeet-like wild bird which will breed with our little budgie and produce viable offspring. We used the word *hybrid* for convenience in describing color inheritance in parakeets. The proper scientific word for a bird with recessive genes which are masked by dominant genes is *heterozygous*; the bird which does not carry recessive genes is said to be *homozygous.*

Comprehensive tables of all the possible mating combinations and expectations—a list far too long to be included in such a general book as this—and further material on the genetics of the parakeet may be found in books devoted to breeding these wonderful little birds.

No one has ever succeeded in breeding any other bird with the budgerigar.

Exhibiting

To the person who is considering breeding para- keets for exhibi tion, the best advice I can give is to "stop, look and listen." To be a successful exhibitor you must first be informed. You can study the standard for the ideal budgie, you can look at pic- tures and read books, but that is not enough. Familiarize yourself with budgie shows as a specta- tor, attending a number of them before you actually enter your bird. Compare the winners with the stan- dard, and if there is any- thing you don't understand ask the judge or one of the old-timers you are sure to meet at any show.

Have a clear under- standing of what is expected of you and your bird. Qualities like size, shape, condition, balance, deportment, shape of head, color, wing markings, etc., all are consid- ered and rated on a point scale. Your bird will be judged on his behavior and poise as well as his ability to reveal his best points. A good bird who "stages" well often wins out over a better bird that does not exhibit itself to advantage. Your bird will be required to conduct himself with dignity while

This opaline cobalt has excellent markings, great color and style, and is fit for exhibition.

93

This is a drawing from the standard and shows an ideal opaline violet hen budgie.

strangers--the judges--examine him minutely.

To achieve all this requires the ultimate in patient breeding and training.

If you decide to go ahead with it, the first thing you will want to do is to join a local budgerigar society, to find out when and where local shows will be held. I suggest that you write to the American Budgerigar Society for information about groups in your locality.

STANDARD FOR THE IDEAL BUDGERIGAR

Condition: This is essential. If a bird is not in condition, he should never be considered.

Type: Gracefully tapered from nape of neck to tip of tail, with an approximately straight back line and a rather deep curved chest. The bird should be perfectly balanced and convey the impression of being well and evenly proportioned.

Length: The ideal British length is 8.5 inches from crown of head to tip of the tail. American judges frequently consider the ideal bird to be a little smaller than this.

Head: Large, round, wide and symmetrical when viewed from any angle; curvature of skull commencing at cere, to lift outward and upward, continuing in one graceful sweep over the top and base of head.

Beak: Set well into face.

Eyes: Bold and bright, positioned well away from front, top and back skull.

Neck: Short and wide when viewed from either side or front.

Wings: Well braced, carried just above the cushion of the tail and not crossed.

The ideal wing length is 3.75 inches from the butt to the tip of the longest primary flight.

Tail: Straight and tight with two long tail feathers.

Position: Steady on the perch at an angle of 30 degrees from the vertical, looking fearless and natural.

Mask and spots: Mask to be clear, deep and wide, ornamented by six evenly spaced large round throat spots, the outer two being partially covered at the base of the cheek patches, the size of the spots to be in proportion to the rest of the make-up of the bird. Spots

can be either too large or too small.

Legs and feet: Legs should be straight and strong, with two front and

How times have changed! These were champion birds in 1955!

The ideal light green cock from a drawing of the standard.

This small yellow face sky blue lacks exceptional qualities, but it has lots of good points.

two rear toes and claws firmly gripping the perch.

Markings: Wavy markings on cheek, head, neck, back and wings to stand out clearly.

Color: Clear and level and of an even shade.

SCALE OF POINTS

When judged, the total point scoring (except for opalines, cinnamons, albinos, and a few rare varieties) adds up to a hundred (perfection) and is scaled like this: Size, shape, condition, balance––30; Deportment and wing carriage––15; Size and shape of head––20; Color––15; Mask and spots––15; Wing markings––5.

96

Conclusion

This is an excellent bird as a light green yellow wing.

Of course you don't *have* to breed your parakeet, you don't *have* to enter him in exhibits. If you are content with just one or two at home with you, that is sufficient, and you will be among the vast majority of parakeet owners.

He offers tropical-flower beauty and responds to your affection. What more could you want? There are stories about people who bought or bred a parakeet to harmonize with the colors of their home. What usually happened was that once the parakeet was installed, home decor was always matched to *him*. There may be little truth in this fable, but it does illustrate the point that many people buy budgies for little or no reason and then find a thousand reasons never to part with them.

Index